Keep Life Sweet!

Honey Beth Wiggs

2-2-17

# Life is Sweeter with Honey

# Life is Sweeter with Honey

## How to Create a Joy Filled Life

Honey Beth Wiggs

**Life Is Sweeter with Honey: How to Create a Joy Filled Life**
Published by First Avenue Press
Raleigh, NC



Library of Congress Control Number: 2016960468

Wiggs, Honey Beth, Author

ISBN: 978-0-9983800-0-1

FAMILY & RELATIONSHIPS / Parenting / Motherhood
SELF-HELP / Personal Growth / Happiness

QUANTITY PURCHASES: Schools, companies, professional groups, clubs, churches, and other organizations may qualify for special terms when ordering quantities of this title. For information, email Info@LifeIsSweeterWithHoney.com.

Dedicated to Dale Wiggs,
Kim and Nathan Fronczak,
Jonathan and Sydney Wiggs,
Austin Wiggs, and Ashlyn Wiggs
for making this crazy adventure of life
sweeter than I ever imagined.

# Contents

# Introduction

## That One Catalyst Moment

I came that they may have and enjoy life,
and have an abundance (to the full, till it overflows).
John 10:10, Amplified Bible

EVERYONE EXPERIENCES AT LEAST ONE DEFINING catalyst moment in life: a moment that causes that person to do an about-face and change direction. Whether the change is a decision on health, lifestyle, career, or family, it can always be traced back to that one defining moment in time when clarity was born. For me, that catalyst moment is burned into my heart and soul forever and is what drives me today to live the life I have chosen. I made a decision to release what people thought I should do and how I should do it, and to replace it with a way to embrace the fullness of life and to center life around what matters most. I chose to drizzle the "sweetness of honey" into every nook and cranny of daily living. My life is full of memorable experiences, and I long to leave a legacy of health, family, adventure, and joy.

I was morbidly obese, 250 to 320 pounds, for about twenty-five years of my life. I know what the deep hurt and scars of being obese are all about. I know how it feels to believe that you have nothing to offer people because of the way you look. I know that being the life of the party is a false front for all the deep hurt inside. I know what it's like to struggle to do fun activities with the family such as horseback riding, roller-skating, swimming, hiking, etc. I couldn't even lift my leg to get on the back of a motorcycle with my husband, Dale. One painful memory was in a boat, on a lake, with my family. I remember the day well. It was 100°F in the middle of July. Everyone was in the water cooling off, and I was sitting in the boat with my life jacket on, sweating profusely, wishing I were in the water too. But I had to consider the ramifications. I knew that it would take an army to help a wet 320-pound woman climb back into the boat. I did not have enough strength to do it on my own. My husband would stand in the boat pulling on my arms while my two teenage children would push me from behind. It would be humiliating!

I also know what it is like to stand in line for a roller coaster and scan the crowds to see if there are people bigger getting on the ride. It is terrifying to think that you will be kicked off the roller coaster because you are too large for the safety harness to close. You stand in line engulfed in fear, sweating because your heart rate is increased because of anxiety. Then one day it happened: I will never forget that moment—the moment when the attendant gave me an uncomfortable, sheepish look and explained that I would have to leave the ride while hundreds of eyes watched me slowly get up and walk out the exit. I felt incredibly humiliated, not for myself, but for my husband. So many thoughts flooded my mind in a matter of seconds, including, "What must he be thinking? How does this make him feel? Is he embarrassed to be with me? Does this make him love me less?" And yet, as immeasurably humiliating as that experience was, it was not my catalyst moment.

When I was a young girl, I dreamed of getting married, having kids, and being a homemaker, the typical "happy ever after" scenario. I met my husband while on vacation in Atlantic Beach, North Carolina. I was vacationing from Maryland with my dad, brother, sister, and girlfriend. Dale was with his two young children, Kim and Jonathan. It was on the Fourth of July, 1991, and it was one of the most interesting turns of events in my life. Let's say that God divinely orchestrated our meeting. I moved to North Carolina in August 1991, and we married on October 16, 1993. As much as I loved my stepchildren, I longed for children of my own, children that would call me "Mommy."

Dale and I tried to get pregnant during those first ten years of marriage, and nothing was working. We were raising his two children at the time, and our lives were pretty busy. I finally went to the doctor to receive some assistance in getting pregnant. I can't remember the exact words that the doctor said, but what I heard was, "You are too fat to have a baby. Go lose weight." I felt like saying, "Well, thank you very much. I didn't know that. And what am I supposed to do?" As deeply hurtful as that conversation was, and despite my feeling of being worthless and incapable of having children, that was still not my catalyst moment.

I set off on a journey to lose weight. I did several yo-yo diets, manipulating my body to see results. I was not healthy; I was just able to lose weight. In a period of two years, I was able to lose a hundred pounds and get pregnant. As a matter of fact, I didn't even know I was pregnant until I was fourteen weeks into the pregnancy!

I knew something was not right because I couldn't stop eating. I remember a wedding we attended a few days before I figured out I was pregnant. We were at Carowinds theme park, in South Carolina, riding roller coasters on a Friday and were attending a wedding on Saturday. The wedding reception was the best reception I ever remembered, probably because of the extreme buffet of food.

There was a shrimp station, beef station, chicken station, pasta station, dessert station, and so on. I kid you not; I probably ate five pounds of shrimp, five pounds of beef, five pounds of chicken, and five pieces of cake! After that, we went back to our hotel room, and guess what? I ordered a large Papa John's ham and pineapple pizza and ate it all! I took a pregnancy test a few days later and was overjoyed beyond belief. As much as I was excited to finally realize that my dreams of being a mom were going to come true, that was still not my catalyst moment.

Every Saturday night and Sunday afternoon, Dale's mom would cook a family meal. Some weekends we would go over on both Saturday night and Sunday after church. It was a highly anticipated family time for everybody. One night, we were having conversations about life. Dale's mom and sister were trying to prepare me for what life was going to be like after I had my sweet baby boy. I kept talking about how excited and nervous I was about this long-awaited blessing. These two sweet women were imparting wisdom to me from their years of beautiful experience as moms. But one sentence changed the course of my life forever. It was not meant in harm, and I know that, but nonetheless, it was the one, crystal clear, most defining moment in my entire life: my catalyst moment.

"You know, once you have that baby, you will not be able to do all the things you do now," they told me.

In the first ten years of our marriage, Dale and I had done our best to enjoy our unique family with the resources we had available. I have always loved to travel. I have many friends who call me a gypsy. We made sure that we enjoyed as much time together taking day trips and as many vacations as we possibly could. At the time I became pregnant, Jonathan and Kim were pretty much older and on their own.

My heart sank when I heard those words from Dale's mom and

sister. Was my life going to stop? Was the one thing I had waited all my life to have happen going to cause my life to be stale and boring? Was I going to feel like I was in jail?

I went home and thought, "What makes you think that we will not be able to travel, enjoy life, and have fun just because I have a baby?" I think part of my sinful mind wanted to say, "Well, let me just show you what our life can look like!" And so it began—a burning desire to prove you can make a purposeful choice to enjoy life to the fullest.

I had my beautiful baby boy, Brian Austin, on December 9, 2002. After three weeks, we went on a four-day vacation to Williamsburg, Virginia. I needed to know for myself that I could do this. I could travel, I could do it on a budget, and I could have fun with the baby and not give up the dreams of creating experiences and memories that last a lifetime.

In October 2003, Dale and I went on a New England cruise to celebrate our tenth wedding anniversary. I was five months pregnant with my daughter and had left my eight-month-old son with my extremely close and gracious girlfriend, Josie, in Maryland. While we were away, Austin got very sick, and Josie had to take him to a pediatric urgent care. This was back in the days when it cost almost five dollars a minute to call home from a cruise liner. I never felt more helpless in my life. I was hundreds of miles away, out at sea, and could not get back to my sick baby. If you are a parent, I'm sure you can imagine that horrible feeling. Helplessness. Misery. Needless to say, it was the worst cruise/anniversary ever! That was another defining moment in our lives. My husband and I both decided instantly that we would never travel without our children ever again.

In March 2004, I had my precious baby girl, Faith Ashlyn. When Ashlyn was nine months old, our family went on a cruise. I love cruising as a family vacation, and we will talk more about that later.

All four of our children were there, as were nieces and nephews and Dale's sister and mom. We had a blast, and that family get-together set the course for many years of an adventurous life.

My catalyst moment, although I didn't see it at the time, was the cornerstone of so much good in my life. You, too, can create a beautiful, joy filled life. All it takes is a decision and action. The benefits in your soul, life, and family will last a lifetime and leave a legacy of joy and adventure.

I myself have been able to do more than I ever dreamed possible on that hundred-degree day in July when I couldn't get in the water to cool off. In 2007, we were able to "vacation" for the equivalent of seven months out of the year. We made a choice of what we wanted and made a plan for how to accomplish it. It is now 2016, and my children are thirteen and twelve. They have been on many cruises, flown across the United States several times, visited almost all of the states, and driven cross-country a few times. And we even decided to live in another state for year. Talk about an adventure!

In 2013, we picked up and decided to live in Austin, Texas, for one year. Because of my work as a certified health coach and the ability to grow my business across America, I was able to allow my husband to step away from his construction business in October 2012. Again, we made a plan to have freedom in our lives. I work from home, so as long as I have a smartphone, I'm good. I also homeschool my children. Now this decision is not for everyone, and honestly, I do NOT love it, but I love the freedom it brings to our family. So these decisions gave us the flexibility to be able to live somewhere else and experience a different culture for a year. We didn't sell our house. We simply rented a townhouse in the Austin area and dove in headfirst with respect to meeting people, fostering friendships, and being relational. To this day, we all believe it was the best year of our lives. Just ask my children!

My life motto is this: Suck every minute out of life because we are not guaranteed tomorrow. Life is short. Don't miss out on the adventure set before you. Yes, that's right! Adventure. Every day starts with the anticipation of fresh starts, new ideas, and most importantly, hope. And the biggest blessing is that each day ends the same way, with hope.

What about you? Have you had that catalyst moment yet? If you have, wonderful. What are you doing with it? Have you set the course for a new direction, a new vision for your life? What wonderful things do you want to accomplish? Have you made an action plan on how to get there? Have you shared your dreams with other family members or friends? This step can feel scary and uncomfortable. However, it will certainly keep you accountable for your desired outcome. There is nothing like having people watch you as an example for what they might do, or wait expectantly for your marvelous revelations to come to light to spur them on to greatness.

If you have not had your catalyst moment, maybe this book will bring that moment for you. Are you struggling with feeling like you have no meaning or purpose in your life? Do you feel as if you are caught in a maze or are oscillating in a cycle of daily activities with no hope of change? Are you afraid of waking one day and realizing your children are grown and then having regrets for not spending more time with them? Are you wishing you could make more memories now before it is too late? Maybe this book will awaken a desire to center your life around what matters most. Maybe you will gain a clear vision for what it could look like to live "full out" with amazing experiences that will create memories for your family while you are molding and shaping the lives of a future generation. My true and genuine wish is to equip and empower you to live the life that you were created to live. And not simply to just live it, but to enjoy life to the fullest extent—a life sweetened with honey, a joy filled life.

### STARTING POINT—WHERE DOES OUR JOY COME FROM?

*I have told you these things, that My joy and delight may be in you and that your joy and gladness may be a full measure and complete and overflowing.*

*John 15:11, Amplified Bible Classic Edition*

Before we go any further, I want to make sure that we are clear on my starting point. My faith in Jesus Christ, the Son of the Living God, as my Lord and Savior is what drives me. It is my North Star. So everything that I share will come from that as my central being and focus point. You may or may not share the same view, but I think it is important moving forward to understand where the groundwork comes from. We have to have a firm cornerstone in place before we can build anything. Whether it is a house, building, self, or family, the foundation on which we are building needs to be firm.

### ENJOY THE JOURNEY

*God directed me to teach you to observe [the commandments]... so that you may enjoy long life.*

*Deuteronomy 6:1–2, New International Version*

Enjoy. Long life. Wow! What hope we have in hearing that. Living a joy filled life is not something we *do*. It is a journey into who we *become*. Once we can master the art of choosing joy in every circumstance, our new and refreshed outlook on life is what drives us to live with meaning, purpose, and excellence every single day.

Do you realize that you have the opportunity to shape a healthy family environment? Let that sink in for a moment. As mothers, we hold the keys to a successful family unit. How we respond to circumstances, how we relate to our husbands, how we nurture our children, the relationships we have, and most importantly, how we care for ourselves all set the tone for a healthy family.

Your life is a journey. Your health is a journey. Raising children is a journey. Your career is a journey. Everything we do is a journey, and we have a choice to find joy in every aspect of life. I can promise you this: choosing joy is a whole lot more fun than choosing frustration, aggravation, and victimization.

In 2009, a study of over seventy-three thousand Japanese men and women found that those who had a strong connection to their ikigai (sense of purpose) tended to live longer than those who didn't. *New York Times* best-selling author Dan Buettner has similar claims. He writes that the two most vulnerable times in a person's life are the first twelve months after birth and the twelve months following retirement.

I share these with you to show and encourage you to enjoy the in-between time! Enjoy the everyday moments of life so that you live with no regrets. If I was to die today, I would not have one single regret about how I've lived my life. I have enjoyed immeasurable time with my husband, my children, my grandchildren, my extended family, and my friends. I have built a life that affords me no regrets. That doesn't mean that I haven't made bad decisions. I have most certainly screwed up from time to time—haven't always chosen joy—but I live with no regrets and keep moving forward. After all, life is a journey.

**VISION**

The journey of a joy filled life does not have to be difficult. Actually, it can be quite easy. There's one simple thing that needs to be put in place: a vision. Not a thought or picture in your head of what life could be like, but a clear, purposeful, well-thought-out, written-down vision. Remember, a goal that is not written down stays a dream. Put it to pen and paper. When there is a lack of vision, we don't have any direction. Do you think you have a clear understanding of the vision of what your family is seeking to become? Would you encourage your family to discuss what the vision of your family is and what the family is doing to fulfill it? One of the most important things you can become aware of is your current reality. If you have a clear understanding of where you want to go (what you desire to achieve) and where you are now, then the rest is easy. Honestly. All it takes is action steps. And guess what? I'm here to help you with that.

The first thing we will do together in part 1 is learn how to dream again. This is a lost art form for adults, and I desire to awaken the sweet joy of having a vision for your family. After the vision is in place, we will explore why doing such exercises is important in part 2. In part 3, we will walk through ways to make the vision a reality. I will give details on how to implement all the great things you desire to accomplish in part 4. Finally, in part 5, I challenge you to create your own action plan.

Living a joy filled, sweet life you cherish with your family, with no regrets, can be a reality.

## Disclaimer

Before we get started, I want to prepare you for something that can be unbelievably freeing and feel very unnatural at the same time. In the chapters to come, I will invite you to do things that may be outside of your comfort zone. From my experience, magic always happens when I am outside my comfort zone. You may hear things differently, be asked to think about things in a new way, or read an idea that is totally foreign to your way of thinking. Please don't shut down; instead, stay open to the glorious journey that could unfold like a peacock spreading its magnificent fan of coverts.

I want you to know—it is absolutely OK to be uncomfortable. My only desire is that you do not close yourself off to a spark, an idea, or a glimmer of revitalized hope and renewed vision of what might happen if—. I've said it before, and I'll say it again: life is a journey. We have beautiful mountaintop experiences followed by some valleys. As wonderful as the mountaintop experiences are, we need the valleys so that we can learn and grow. The more we learn and grow, the higher and higher our mountaintop experiences are, allowing us to see further and further into the beauty of what life can become.

Are you ready to dig in? Take a deep breath, and let's get started! In the next section, we will go through a few exercises to help you get clarity on your vision so that you can take the steps you need for the dream to become reality.

# WHAT IF?

*You are like clay in the potter's hands.*
*Jeremiah 18:6, Easy-to-Read Version*

WHAT IF YOU COULD MOLD AND form your life as if it were a piece of clay? What if you looked at life as a gift that is ready to be unwrapped and given to others? What if you created a life that is centered around what matters most? What if your life was the sweetest form of soul-satisfying joy you could ever imagine?

It can happen. There is a famous quote by Walt Disney: "If you can dream it, you can do it." Walt then goes on to say, "Always remember that this whole thing was started with a dream and a mouse." I love that! The happiest place on earth began with a dream and a mouse. The steps that Walt used are the same steps you can use to live a life filled with sweet joy. It all starts with a dream followed by an action plan outlining what to do and how to do it. Let's start dreaming.

# 1 The Dream Date

"For I know the plans I have for you," declares the Lord, "
...plans to give you hope and a future."
Jeremiah 29:11, New International Version

HOPE. THAT IS A POWERFUL WORD. I love to give people hope—hope for health, awakening hope within our lives, hope for a healthy mindset and total well-being, and hope for a future. Hopes and dreams seem to pair well together. We use the words when referring to the future. We say, "I have so many hopes and dreams for the future" and usually leave the thought right there. Period. Silence. Why?

Why is it when we are young we are filled with hopes and dreams? Even when we are in college or get married, life is a wonderful adventure, and we have so many clear visions for the future. Then something happens. A switch is flipped. Between raising kids, paying bills, and caring for aging parents, our hopes and dreams get smaller and smaller. Sometimes our dreams are for our children, wishing on them what we didn't accomplish or receive. We want their lives to be bigger and better. That's not necessarily a bad thing, but when we do this we tend to live hoping for the future, missing out on the beauty of the now.

Are we scared to say our hopes and dreams out loud because they sound silly coming out of our mouths? Are we afraid of what others might think? Does the thought of criticism for thinking outside of the box and having an adventurous spirit terrify us? Are we scared to write hopes and dreams on paper because that means we might actually have to put some effort into accomplishing a lofty goal? Are we scared to think about the finances and time that might be required? Maybe we feel as if we can't dream anymore? I'm not talking about the dreams that happen when we are in that sweet state of REM sleep, but the dreams that fill our souls, keep our minds spinning and pull us toward joy.

I have a solution for any and all of the above hindrances. Go on a dream date! That's right. Schedule a date to dream. Every January, right after New Year's Eve, Dale and I go on a beautiful "plan-the-year date." This is one of our favorite dates of the year. In a month that can be sometimes depressing, it brings us hope and joy. First, we decide on a beautiful location that has an atmosphere conducive to our dreaming. We make a reservation if necessary. Next, we put it on the calendar. The anticipation of such a great evening is so much fun. I call it "the-getting- ready-to-get-ready" stage. Once the day or evening arrives, we get dressed up so that we feel good about ourselves and head off on our dream date. The most important items to take with you on the date are your calendar and paper and pen.

Once we get settled, it is time for the fun to begin. We open our calendar and make sure the solid events we know are coming up are written in stone. Once the nonnegotiables are done, we can start thinking about what we might want to do leading up to or after that particular event. For example, every October there is a leadership conference we are honored to attend in Sundance, Utah. Our first conversation usually revolves around these questions: How long do we want to stay at the resort? Do we want to fly into Vegas and rent a car? Do we want to roam around California and visit San Francisco, Napa Valley, and Lake Tahoe before the event? Do we want to catch the hot air balloon festival in Albuquerque, New Mexico, after the event? Who do we want to take with us?

We also talk about the super big things that may or may not ever happen. If we could live anywhere for a year, where would it be? Overseas? What mission trip can we take to be a blessing to others during a time of need? My husband is a private pilot. We discuss what his goals are with flying. I was a flute performance major in college. I like to put down performances, trainings, or even recordings I might like to make. Anything that interests us personally.

Another great activity is to ask your children where they would like to go on vacation during the coming year or what fun thing they would want to experience. We usually allow for them to each add at least one event of their choosing to the calendar. One year it was to spend a birthday at Disney World. Great! On the calendar. Another year it was to take a three-month cruise around the world. Not everything makes it onto the calendar for the current year, but we can put it on a calendar for an upcoming year.

In another example, we spent two years dreaming about visiting the islands of Hawaii for the month of December, and now that has become a reality. I desire to travel overseas and spend three to four months touring London, Italy, France, Germany, and Switzerland with my younger kids before they turn sixteen. I have a plan in place for that adventure.

Dale and I have always had great conversations about things we desire to do, places we want to go, and when we want to go. These conversations really drive our energy, not only to give us something to look forward to but also to experience life together as a family. Whenever I think about visiting a certain city or destination, I always envision my family there with me to experience it for the first time. Experiences seem so much richer to me when my heart is full with loved ones around.

The bottom line: dream! Create a vision for your family and have a plan of action. In the chapters ahead, I will guide you through exercises to move you toward a clear vision. I will help you find creative ways to find time and resources to accomplish your goals and tie it all together with a beautiful action plan.

I truly desire for you to live with no regrets, for you to avoid wishing your life away. If there was ever a moment to follow your passion and do something that matters to you and your family, the time is now. Find something you really love to do, an adventure you can't possibly conceive happening that stirs your heart and awakens your soul, and do it with the people you love most. One of the most dangerous and debilitating words in any vocabulary is "tomorrow." Life is short. Let's start on the path of making memories and creating experiences so we can leave a legacy of joy. Master the art of dreaming without boundaries once again.

# 2 How to Dream

> It was the Lord who gave us eyes for seeing
> and ears for hearing.
> Proverbs 20:12, Easy-to-Read Version

THERE ARE TIMES IN OUR LIVES when we gain a vision, a dream, a glimpse of something fantastic that is spoken to us in a still, quiet voice within our soul. I promise you—that voice speaks often. The problem is we don't hear it nearly enough. We have the loud, clanging, overwhelming noise of our to-do list and cries of the heart ringing constantly in our ears.

Have you ever taken the time to sit quietly? Sometimes all it takes is a few minutes to be still. Meditation is a beautiful habit of health. However, I am talking about something a little different. Have you ever given yourself time to sit, purposefully allowing your mind to wander and be divinely led in directions you never imagined? I encourage you to do this exercise. Find a quiet room. Let's keep it real. For some, this might be the bathroom. It doesn't matter. Give yourself five minutes in a quiet room and take a pad of paper and pen. Take a few deep breaths and start to listen—and hear that quiet voice inside your soul. Write down *everything* that comes to your mind. Do this for a few days, even a week. I guarantee you will start to see a pattern, a theme, of what your soul is speaking and the secret desires of your heart.

Some of the most inspirational thoughts I have ever received happened in only a matter of minutes because I allowed myself the permission to think "what if?" Take a few minutes now to be still and quiet for a few minutes and picture yourself in a month, six months, or a year down the road. Where will you be? Who will you be with? What do you want to do? Where do you want to go? Write it down!

Another way I love to awaken my dreaming ability is to visualize by taking into account what others have experienced. I love to flip through magazines while waiting in store lines to check out beautiful destinations. I love to scroll through social media posts while waiting for the kids to finish an activity and be inspired to visit these places. When I have a friend who has come back from a trip, I love to connect with that friend over the phone, a video chat, or a cup of coffee and find out about the friend's favorite experiences while away.

Here is a fabulous idea for awakening your dreaming potential. Have you ever spent an extended period of time having a conversation with a child? As parents, we have the opportunity to do this all the time. Children dream about everything! Their vision for the future has no boundaries. None! It is so refreshing to listen to a child dream, hope, and plan for the future with no restrictions whatsoever. Children have not been jaded by society to think that they can't accomplish their dreams. And on a sidenote, we as parents have the opportunity to foster and grow those beautiful hopes for their future.

We have a wonderful opportunity to learn from children. If you are the parent of young children, or have grandchildren, or know a friend that has children, use them as your teacher for an extended period of time one day. I would encourage you to ask them a few questions:

- What do you want to be when you grow up?
- Why?
- Where do you want to live when you grow up?
- Why?
- Who do you want to marry when you grow up?
- Why?
- How many children do you want to have?
- Why?

Do you see the pattern? Just ask questions and follow up by asking, "Why?" You will be amazed at how freely children dream and envision their future. They have no restrictions, no restraints, no concerns about money or time. They dream and dream big!

What about you? Now it's your turn. What do you dream about? Do you know how to dream? Do you allow yourself to dream? Do you feel guilty or silly when you allow yourself to dream?

What are the deepest desires of your heart? Do you even allow yourself to go to the place that holds those deepest thoughts and longings? Does it scare you to open that door and dream? The Bible tells us that God knows the deepest desires of our heart (Romans 8:27, *Easy-to-Read Version*). I truly believe that God plants desires within our heart so that He can fulfill them for our joy and His glory.

Take a few minutes to answer the questions below. I want you to spend some time dreaming. And not simply surface dreaming, but digging into detail and dreaming in color!

What would you do if you knew you could not fail?

________________________________________

________________________________________

________________________________________

________________________________________

What do you want for your family?

________________________________________

________________________________________

________________________________________

________________________________________

What do you want to accomplish for yourself?

________________________________________

________________________________________

________________________________________

________________________________________

What experiences would you like to give to your family?

________________________________________

________________________________________

________________________________________

________________________________________

What would you do if time and money were no concern?

Where would you go?

How would you travel there? Car? What type? Plane? What class seating? Boat? What type of stateroom?

Who would you be with?

How long would you be there?

What things would you do while you were there?

What does your personal health look like in one, three, and five years?

What does your family look like in one, three, and five years? Number of kids, adoption, grandkids, where you are living, where the kids are attending school, etc.?

I hope you really took time to answer those questions. Now, let's take a little test. With your answers to those questions, and even some additional inspired thoughts that may have crossed your mind, written down, take a good look at them. Read them over again. If you think that you can easily accomplish a dream or know exactly how you will accomplish it, you may not be dreaming big enough. Does your deepest desire, the thing that excites you the most from the above exercise, scare you when you think about how to accomplish it? Perfect! That is where we want to be—right on the outskirts of our comfort zone. Remember, you don't want your dreams to be stifled by your current reality. You want to hope for the deepest, most precious desires of your heart, which might just start to be awakened within you. Dreaming big is so important for moving forward in a joy filled life.

Before we get into some of the more practical applications for making life a little sweeter, there is one more thing you will need to think about. How do you spend your time? One of the biggest deterrents for people accomplishing their dreams and goals is the feeling of lack of time. Wondering if there are enough hours in the day to accomplish our everyday activities is hard enough, let alone adding ambitious, adventurous goals to the mix. However, time is something that can be found and even multiplied when you approach the search from a creative attitude, as we will see in the next chapter.

# 3 How Do You Spend Your Time?

*...Use your time in the best way you can.*
*Colossians 4:5, Easy-to-Read Version*

IT HAS BEEN MY EXPERIENCE THAT I can feel busy and yet never get anything done. Have you ever said to yourself, "Yes, that would be nice, but I just don't have time." Does that sentence sound like your current reality?

We lose hope and lose focus on what we truly desire because we can't possibly imagine adding one more thing to our already overflowing plate of responsibilities. As a mom, I understand this on many levels. Can you see how that thought can prevent you from dreaming and working with joy to make your dreams a reality? I am here to encourage you. Moving away from busyness and walking toward productivity can happen in a few easy steps and possibly an unconventional train of thought. Time is precious, and when we keep it aligned with our goals without letting it slip through our hands, the sweetness of life can seep into the nooks and crannies of the day.

My good friend Kimberly Alexander is a published author and speaker. Her book series, including *The Results Map* and *The Results Map for Women in Biz,* has great strategies for "making things happen." She is phenomenal at helping people see how they are spending their time. Kimberly helped me understand that we all have the same twenty-four hours in a day, 168 hours in a week, and that I was terribly short on hours and over on activity.

I challenge you to write down all the activities you do throughout the course of one week. List how much time you spend doing every single activity in your day: sleeping, getting ready in the morning, eating breakfast, working, taking care of kids, cleaning, doing laundry, spending quiet time (meditation/prayer), cooking dinner, fulfilling appointments, working out, serving as taxi mom, going to church, resting, spending time with friends, etc. Everything. I think you will be surprised to find that the activities add up to way more than the 168 hours contained in a week. How does that happen? Well, the answer is that you are probably not being as productive with your time as you think you are.

What does this exercise have to do with enjoying life? Again, it is to get a feel for your current reality. Nothing can change if you don't know what needs to change. Here is a real game changer for some of you. This is where my ideas may rub you a little or open total freedom for you. Sometimes we need to make a decision about things that we need to start doing or stop doing while finding creative solutions for both.

When I first started working at my church, I filled a part-time position in the housekeeping department. "Nice, easy, relaxing, mindless, good work," is what I thought to myself. Well, I was entirely wrong. You see, my church was in an old six-story hotel that was open one day and shut down the next. Our church bought it,

350 rooms and bathrooms in all! Cleaning was not quite as easy as I thought. It didn't take long for me to extremely dislike spending my off hours at home scrubbing toilets.

I had to make a decision. I loved working for my church; being around that environment and the income really helped our family. The downside was that I felt like every free moment was spent cleaning my house. My joy and energy at home were being depleted. After talking to a few family members, our aunt Neva agreed to help us out at home. It was a blessing for her and us.

Maybe you work a full-time job and hate to clean your house on the weekend. Is there someone you can bless, someone to hire that could do it for you, even once in a while? What about someone to do yard work, to help with laundry a few hours a week, to grocery shop for you? Think outside the box for creative solutions to help free up some time and energy.

What about things that we want to accomplish or want to do? Consider my sister, June (Buggy as I have always affectionately called her). She runs her own web-design business. When she had her first son, she wanted to continue to nurse and work from home. Every time I would visit her, the baby was in a pouch on her back either sleeping or nursing. While keeping true to her desire to work from home, she realized that the best use of her resources to become more productive was to hire a nanny for a few hours a day—not multitask. In business, sometimes you have to take steps that are counterintuitive. If June had been afraid to spend a little money, she may not have had the freedom to grow her business by leaps and bounds. The nanny became full-time because June had the energy, time, and joy to do what she loved while keeping focused on her vision of family.

## THE MYTH OF MULTITASKING

Multitasking is the most vicious killer of true accomplishments. Time blocking versus multitasking makes all the difference. Multitasking makes you feel spread thin and like you never get anything done. Time blocking makes much more sense. Turn off your phone, get rid of distractions, and become singularly focused for a specific duration. If you block out time to take care of a specific task and only do that task, you will actually become more productive.

There is a huge difference between being busy and being productive. I will never forget the time when I realized my life was totally unintegrated I was at a women's retreat with a wonderful speaker. Cindi Wood, the author of *The Frazzled Female*, helped me realize something pivotal: God calls us to be busy and occupied in our lives. We have opportunities to bring Him glory in our daily activities. What He does not call us to do is to be overly occupied and so busy that we don't have energy to do what He is truly calling us to do.

I had to take a long hard look at my life and was inspired to make some changes. At that point, I was homeschooling very young children, working full-time as an administrative assistant to a pastor, working part-time as a booking agent for a very talented group based out of Nashville, Tennessee, and helping my husband's construction business. Did that just make your head swim? Want to know the funny thing? It felt very normal to me. I felt like I could handle anything, even with one hand behind my back and blindfolded. I had mastered the art of becoming overly occupied and too busy to the point that it looked and felt normal. That realization frightened me. I realized that what I was doing was not healthy for my body, mind, spirit, or family. Just because I could do it didn't mean I should do it. Let that sit for a second.

If you are a type A personality like me, we fill our schedule with busyness and a to-do list so that we can check items off of the list. I love lists! If I had an item that wasn't checked off of my list for the day, I would write it on my list for the next day just so I could check it off then. Somehow, that made me feel like I had accomplished a lot for the day. However, what I have come to learn is that marking things off of a list does not help me accomplish great, huge, gigantic, beautiful, joy filled aspirations. Blocking chunks of time is so much easier! Taking thirty minutes a day to answer phone calls, an hour to respond to e-mails, two hours to do laundry or clean the bathrooms—in other words, blocking time—works better. Trust me! Here is an example from my own personal experience.

Several years ago I felt a story welling up inside of me. My life was so unique—given my past, my adoption, my thoughts—that I had been told I should write a book. I had often thought about a book but didn't know where to begin or what to do. Early in 2016, I had begun to feel this particular book welling up within my soul. I knew it was maturing, preparing to be born. I attempted on several occasions to begin to think about this project. In my time at home and even on vacations, I could not bring myself to think about subject matters, much less write anything down. I knew the only way I was going to be able to focus was to schedule time away, alone, by myself, with nobody else.

After a couple of months of planning, with the agreement of my wonderful husband, who was supporting me every step of the way, I arranged to be gone for three weeks. Yes, we had to put people in place to help everything run like a well-oiled machine, but if I had not taken the time to be alone, I would not have been able to rejuvenate, focus, and think. The blessing? With only one to two focused hours a day over a period of twelve days (I played a lot too), I was able to not only get an outline together but also finish my first and second rough manuscript for this project. I intentionally blocked chunks of time to turn off my phone, open my inspirational readings and previous notes, and do nothing but be led to share what was being placed in my heart in order to encourage and inspire you to live a life sweetened with honey.

Are you overly occupied and too busy? In order to enjoy life, you need to have time to enjoy life.

When you added up your hours, did your weekly total come to over 168? This is a great opportunity to look at what you might need to do to rearrange some priorities. Consider hiring out help to create more time. Consider what things are OK to leave alone for a short period so that you might transfer time to something you will enjoy and your family will enjoy. Plan a chunk of time just for you to rejuvenate. Sometimes I feel it is better to have a messy house and happy family.

To live a joy filled life, you need to allow yourself the opportunity to ask the question, "What if?" Dig into those quiet revelations and dream in such a way that you smile big and broad, and you almost laugh out loud as you contemplate what brings joy to your life. Who you are sharing these experiences with is what can complete your soul's desire. In order to accomplish some of the work to prepare for memorable times, or even for self-preservation, it might take some letting go and hiring out. A reworking of your time can be the opening to the door of opportunities. Don't be scared. A season of "messy" can be followed by a season of blessing!

# WHY DO IT

A happy heart is good medicine and a cheerful mind works healing, but a broken spirit dries up the bones.
Proverbs 17:22, Amplified Bible

IN MY CAREER AS A CERTIFIED health coach, I spend time assisting clients in developing optimal well-being, which includes a healthy body and mind. I think it's important for you to understand the difference between happiness and joy. Happiness is circumstantial while joy is a choice seated deep within the soul. Having a happy heart keeps us centered on the good things in our lives while a joyful mind directs us to a life of gratitude and love. When our heart and mind are not centered, we can dip into the pits of life's drama that wear us down. That is why it is important to be clear on your dreams, to know what you are working to create in order to have energy to live the gloriously sweet lives we are individually called to pursue. So why should you desire to live a life centered around your dreams?

# 4 A Happy Heart

So my heart is happy, and the words I speak are words of joy. Yes, even my body will live with hope...
Acts 2:26, Easy-to-Read Version

## HAPPINESS VERSUS JOY

I WILL NEVER FORGET A QUOTE that I heard in reference to submission. "It is easy to submit to someone until there is a disagreement," Pastor Joel McDaniel said one Sunday. I think about this in relationship to happiness versus joy. It is easy to choose joy until something difficult happens. What will we do? How will we respond?

We hear the words happiness and joy used interchangeably all the time. The meanings seem to intertwine with each other. The dictionary defines happiness as having joy and joy as being happy. I believe that these two words have very different meanings. One is situation driven and the other soul driven.

Happiness is dependent on our circumstances. As long as life is going the way we want, we are happy. As long as we get our way, we are happy. As long as we have plenty of money, we are happy. And the list goes on. While there is nothing wrong with being happy, happiness is not something that we are promised. Life is hard. We have disappointments. Happiness is something that most people search for and seldom consistently hold on to. That is because happiness is fleeting. Sometimes we catch it, and sometimes we don't, and that can really affect our mind-set and spirit. When things are hard, what happens? That is the biggest difference happiness has with joy.

Joy is something that we are promised. Joy is everlasting. It is our spiritual birthright from Christ. It is not circumstantial. Joy is a choice we make in the difficult moments. It is how you see a situation, how you react and respond to good and bad circumstances. Joy comes from the innermost being of our heart. Our hearts can be full because joy comes from Christ, and Christ never changes.

Life seems cruel sometimes. Horrible things happen: the death of a spouse, child, or parent; cancer; car accidents. The list goes on. There are so many things entering our lives on a daily, sometimes moment-by-moment, basis that can steal our happiness.

There are two things that I believe are for certain. One is that we will all have trials:

"My brothers and sisters, think of the various tests you encounter as occasions for joy. After all, you know that the testing of your faith produces endurance. Let this endurance complete its work so that you may be fully mature, complete, and lacking in nothing." (James 1:2–4, *Common English Bible)*.

The second is that trials are seasonal. They will not last forever:

"There's a season for everything and a time for every matter under the heavens: a time for giving birth and a time for dying, a time for planting and a time for uprooting what was planted…a time for tearing down and a time for building up, a time for crying and a time for laughing, a time for mourning and a time for dancing." (Ecclesiastes 3:1–4, *Common English Bible).*

Yes, you will suffer for a short time. But after that, God will make everything right. He will make you strong. He will support you and keep you from falling. "He is the God who gives all grace. He chose you to share in his glory in Christ. That glory will continue forever." (1 Peter 5:8–10, *Easy-to-Read Version).*

We have the ability to choose joy, to choose gratitude, to choose to be thankful. When we come from a place of gratitude and joy, the world seems to be brighter and our outlook on life, including what we want to accomplish, becomes clearer.

**PHYSICAL HEALTH**

I grew up hearing the phrase "A happy heart is a healthy heart." When we think about a healthy heart, two things come to mind: physical health and the health of our spirit. Both are dependent on each other. When they work together in harmony, the result is a glorious duet in our song of joyful living.

Just as a conductor leads the orchestra to not simply play the notes on a page but make beautiful music, we have the opportunity to lead our body to not simply survive but thrive through life. If we care for our body, the way it was designed to be fueled and treated, then we will have the energy, clarity, desire, and joy to live out our lives with the meaning and purpose designed for us. I feel health is the starting point for all joy filled living. If you don't have your health (physical and mental), you don't have anything to give to others.

Creating health can be hard. Being unhealthy can be hard. Choose your hard. For over twenty-five years I lived in morbid obesity, going from 250 to 320 pounds. I definitely know what it is like to live to eat and not eat to live. When I was 320 pounds, I would wake up in the morning and skip breakfast. I wasn't crazy about breakfast or the typical breakfast foods. I would much rather wait until the Golden Corral next to my office opened up for lunch at 11 a.m. You see, when I woke up every morning, all I could do was think about what I was going to eat for lunch. After about an hour of feasting at the buffet, I would go back to work and start thinking about what we were going to do for dinner. At 4:00 p.m., I would call in an order for two extra large and one medium ham and pineapple pizzas from Papa John's across the street. Unbeknownst to my family, I would eat the medium pizza on the way home from work and share the two extra large pizzas with them for dinner. I felt many things after such a day—sick to my stomach, regret, and guilt. My eating habits were affecting my physical health and mental health.

I know what it is like to suffer from the inside out. I know what it is like to put up a front and pretend to be happy when you are miserable on the inside. I know what it is like to have physical pain from carrying so much weight. I know what it's like to not have energy to do the fun things your family desires. What changed? My "why." It was no longer good enough to not care about myself and be addicted to food. I knew what I wanted from my life, and what I was doing was not going to allow me to accomplish my hopes and dreams of having children. Finding the program that assisted me to change the trajectory of my life was one of my biggest blessings and allowed me to realize what true health looks like.

Optimal health is not a number on a scale. How can you weigh the feeling of total well-being? It is not a diet/cheat mentality. Optimal health is making daily decisions to move yourself forward while having joy in your journey. It is having a healthy body, healthy mind, healthy spirit, and healthy finances. It is having a heart of gratitude and thankfulness that gives you total well-being. I never want to go back to the way I used to feel. Ever! That is why I love supporting others in their journey. Living an optimally healthy life is addictive and can open the door for new experiences, such as incorporating family time and healthy cooking into everyday life.

## SPIRIT OF HEALTH

To me, the spirit of health is exemplified, and even magnified, in gathering around the table as a family. Meals bring people together. A meal is where laughter happens most. It is where conversations unwrap the gifts of the day, and connections of the heart are made over food, interaction, and love. It is where celebrations occur, plans are made, and projects are completed, and it is the information center of the home. My friend, Frances Knott George described this feeling best in one of her Facebook posts:

> Thirty-one years ago, newlyweds Craig and Fran purchased an unfinished oak table and four chairs for our new home. When our family numbered 5, we added two more chairs. After birthday breakfasts and dinners, countless cups of spilled milk, creating exquisite homemade Valentine's, eyes stinging over peanut butter and jelly sandwiches after swimming in the pool, candles pushed in the breakfast birthday Krispy Kreme doughnut and endless hours of laughter and love and unrushed mornings, afternoons and evenings... The old oak table is going upstairs and being replaced with a new and wonderfully enormous table for our precious and gigantic family dinners. New memories with our 25+ member family here in town will begin around this new family centerpiece. Oh the fun that will be had...a new generation of milk spillers, Krispy Kreme birthday doughnuts, candles, homemade Valentine's and laughter. Oh life around my table. What an immeasurably happy part of my home.

Sitting down together at a meal is certainly a great place to start or end the day, but don't forget there is more to the event. Cooking together can be an enjoyable way to share a spirit of happy health. What an awesome opportunity to enlist the help of your family in picking out healthy recipes, menus, and shopping lists. Start with just your family dinner. If you don't have at least one meal together as a family every day, without electronics, let that be your first goal. If you have children, let them help plan, prepare, and partake in the aspects of a great meal. Many families sit to have dinner but don't talk. Be a great listener and ask questions. Instead of asking an open-ended question such as "How was your day?"—only to receive a "Fine" in response—ask, "What was the best part of your day?" And by now you should know what the follow-up question to that is. You guessed it! "Why?"

I love asking the question "Why?" I recently played my flute for a group of senior citizens while they were having lunch. I took requests for their favorite hymns. In order to give myself time to look up the hymn they requested, I always asked why it was their favorite hymn. Oh my word! To hear the stories about how these great hymns of faith impacted people's lives was overwhelming. It got to the point where I just couldn't wait to hear what they were going to say. Asking "why" is a beautiful thing and allows you to be an active listener. When we interact with people and are totally present in the conversation—not only hearing their words, but also their heart—is when we have an opportunity to connect on a deeper level.

It is important to keep the spirit of our heart healthy as much as our body. The more we can become a person who has energy to serve, the bigger our heart will be to serve, allowing our spirit to be full. If we are living a life of gratitude and love, even when we are hit by hard things—bad things, unimaginable things—they won't derail us. Even though we may hurt for a time, we have an opportunity to choose joy, which will lead to a longer, healthier life.

**FAMILY TRAVEL**

Our hearts are never more unified in happiness of spirit than when we go on adventures together. Whether it is for a day, week, or month, travel is the space we put in between things so that our life doesn't jumble together into one indecipherable mess. It gives us breathing room, time to think and self-reflect, without losing our standing in the world. And when we look back for memories, the trips we take are like anchors or chapter titles helping us distinguish one year from the next. I recently read about the brain and how ideas are moved from short-term to long-term memory. And I've read that our adult lives seem to go by so much faster than our childhood lives because they're marked by fewer monumental moments.

My sweet friend Kim Fiske went on a thirteen-day, twenty-five hundred-plus mile journey cross-country in a truck camper with her husband, Joe. This is what she had to say about the experience:

> When I asked Joe today what his favorite part of the trip was he said – "The best part was just being with you...alone...for all this time... And also seeing all the great things WITH you." (I know...all of you women just went "ahhhh.") He had traveled a lot of this road several times alone by truck and motorcycle. I decided to go on this trip mainly to "buy his chairs" (You have to know the movie Phenomenon with John Travolta to understand the context.) - but I was equally, if not more, "filled-up" by the experience than he was. I now will only have these memories.

Travel gives us those moments and fills the space we need to enjoy future experiences. Spending time together with your family in a hotel room can be one of the sweetest experiences ever. Don't get me wrong; there can be a lot of aggravation with it as well, but again, it's what you make of it. If you choose joy in all circumstances, it can be a beautiful experience that your family will never forget.

We spend so much time together in hotel rooms as a family of four, sometimes three or four weeks at a time, that when we get home, the kids will want to cuddle for hours in our queen-size bed together. They will want to lay with us and talk. We end up having family Bible time smushed on our bed together. They will want to sleep in our bedroom with us or in the living room on the couch that is adjacent to our bedroom. Travel has the potential to form a physical, heartstring bond that strengthens your family unit far beyond any other activity you could do.

My prayer is that you realize the difference between happiness and joy, the importance of physical health, the health of your spirit, and the value of vacations and family time together—and see it happening for yourself. My hope is to empower you to believe that you can enjoy time together as a family unit. We all need time to unplug, reconnect, and recharge. There is nothing that draws us closer together in unity then focusing on loving and enjoying one another, being 100 percent fully present with the ones you love.

Above all, be careful what you think because your thoughts control your life.
Proverbs 4:23, Easy-to-Read Version

IN MY OPINION, A CHEERFUL MIND is always seeking new ways to grow personally, is being exercised and focused, and pays attention to self-care. It is true that our thoughts can control our life. Our thoughts can make us sick or help us heal. They can drive us toward despair or toward hope. We have the power to control our mind, so what we put in is what will come out.

## PERSONAL DEVELOPMENT

Personal development is an attitude of improvement. True personal growth and development starts with making the decision that one of the most important things you can do in life is to constantly improve and become a better version of your former self. I believe that investing in personal development will move you closer to your goal by leaps and bounds. You have an opportunity to improve your awareness of not only yourself but also others you interact with on a daily basis. This area of a cheerful mind is not something you mark off of your to-do list; it is who you become over time. Growth is a journey, not a destination.

With a plethora of books in every bookstore centered around a healthy mind, the key aspects are mental, physical, social, emotional, and spiritual growth. I enjoy the benefits of growing my mind. Leaders are readers. I read. A lot. I encourage you to read. A few authors who are experts in this field are Jim Rohn, Stephen R. Covey, Zig Ziglar, Grant Cardone, John Maxwell, and my personal favorite, Og Mandino.

Expand your mind in areas that interest you and excite you, areas that you want to improve. Ernest Hemingway said, "There is nothing noble in being superior to your fellow man; true nobility is being superior to your former self." A most helpful way to improve yourself is to become mindful every day in every way possible.

## EXERCISING YOUR MIND

Many people go through life mindless. Think about it. Have you ever mindlessly eaten? For example, you make a sandwich for your children and cut off the crust. What do you do with the crust? Eat it? There is just one bite of leftover dinner on your child's plate. What do you do? Eat it? When baking, do you ever lick the bowl or spoons? Let's take driving as another example. Do you take the same route to work, school, and appointments every day? Do you find yourself in deep thought, only to realize, "Wow! How did I get here?" Much of our day is spent on autopilot, and unless you make a concerted effort to change things up, you will stay that way.

John C. Maxwell once said, "You'll never change your life until you change something you do daily. The secret of your success is found in your daily routine." I want to challenge you to turn off the autopilot and take full control of the wild joys of life. Drive a different route to work once a week. Take the back roads. Brush your teeth or write your name with the opposite hand. For heaven's sake, even wear your clothes inside out one day and see how it feels to be a rebel. Do things differently to exercise your brain and be creative.

A cheerful mind is also in a place of contentment. Remember our conversation about happiness versus joy? When we can come from a place of gratitude and thanksgiving, our mind has the opportunity to release stress in our body. I believe it is better to be kind than to be right. Whenever we feel anxious, angry, and frustrated, taking a few deep breaths will help send oxygen to the brain, helping us to think more clearly. One question that I like to ask myself, often in the midst of what might seem chaos, is, "Will this matter tomorrow, next week, next month, or a year from now?" If the answer is "No," then do like the Disney character Elsa and "Let it go."

## SELF-CARE

Here is another one of those moments that you may have to prepare yourself for. Self-care is essential for a healthy mind. Ladies, this is especially for you. As mothers, no matter how old we are, or how old our kids are, we always seem to put the needs of everyone else first. While that is a noble and good thing, without the right insertion of self-care, you will be of no use to anyone. What is self-care? Anything that relaxes you, calms you, and rejuvenates you.

For a couple of years, I would go and get a two-hour massage every week. It was what I needed to be the best me for my family. Just because you decide to do something to help yourself doesn't mean you have to do it forever. Find what works for you right now and make a commitment, no matter how small, to set time aside to renew, rejuvenate, and refresh. I really encourage you, when blocking time in your day, to block a little for you, and make it a priority. You are not an afterthought. The whole feel and flow of your house is dependent on you, your attitude, your health.

It is OK to think about yourself. It is OK to take a little time every day to put yourself before others. It is OK to care about your state of mind and personal well-being. Take the time to care for yourself in a way that gives you energy for everyone else and the things God is calling you to do. If you need to make some adjustments in your eating habits, do it. If you need to go to the gym, do it. If you need to meditate, walk with a friend, play your musical instrument, sing, dance, get a manicure or pedicure, go for a massage, or sit and play a game on your computer or smartphone, do it. It's OK. Whatever it is, plan to do something every day that will give you a happy heart and cheerful mind. By taking time for you, your body will have the ability to heal and be stronger physically and mentally.

## HEALING

*Be still...*

*Psalm 46:10a, New International Version*

Rest. We all need rest. Rest is how we heal. It is how we repair. It is how we renew. It is the way we were created to function and is the example set before us by God. If He needed rest, then why do we think we don't need rest? What exactly does rest do for us?

Sleep is the only time when the body can repair and renew from the day's activities. It is the time when your body shuts down and in essence says, "OK. It's time to repair all the damage from the day so that you can wake up for tomorrow feeling alert and refreshed." While sleep is needed for our body to repair, rest is needed for our body to relax.

I have experienced what an overload of stress and lack of rest can do to the body. I have experienced adrenal fatigue, in which your adrenal glands are shot because of an overload of stress in your body. I was suffering from several physical conditions that I could do nothing about. There was no drug, no quick fix, that would instantly cure this ailment. The only thing I could do was start on a replenishing regimen and enter a season of rest. I had to make a decision to let go of some things, to not be so controlling, to stop stressing over things that didn't matter, and simply rest.

What exactly did that look like, this season of rest? I needed to allow my husband to take the lead on a few things in our household. What that meant for me was to not be concerned that chores were not done the way I would do them. It meant hiring people to take care of a few extra details in my household and business.

Resting for you may be something as simple as a long hot bath or a few hours a week of nothing but alone time. It could mean having your husband take the kids to the park for an hour so that you could sit in silence. You may decide to spend one night a month at a hotel—by yourself. Rest can look different for different people. There is no right or wrong answer for what that will look like for you. Are you in need of scheduling rest into your day or week?

When you can care for yourself, placing an emphasis on living in the now with your family while keeping one foot in the future, then you are in full position to make extraordinary things bloom into beauty within your life. By doing so, you will allow yourself to have a happy heart and joyful mind. Then you will be able to concentrate on the memorable experiences in life that you can enjoy with your family. Another great benefit of rest and self-care is that it will give you energy to invest in others as you build meaningful relationships.

# Part Three

## WHERE TO START

Do nothing from selfish ambition or conceit, but in humility
count others more significant than yourselves.
Let each of you look not only to his own interests,
but also to the interests of others.
Philippians 2:3–4, English Standard Version

THE WAY I SEE IT, THERE are two key components necessary to walk the journey of a joy filled life: relationships and freedom. We were created to be relational beings. When we take time to invest in the lives of others, we open the door for rich blessings deep within our soul. Friendships within our family and our sphere of influence can be one of the sweetest drips of honey into our lives. Having the freedom to center our lives around the importance of relationships is a true gift. To have time and resources to give to others brings about a greater return on our investments of the soul than we could ever imagine.

# 6 Family and Friends

> Then the Lord God said, "I see that it is not good for the man to be alone. I will make the companion he needs, one just right for him."
>
> Genesis 2:18, Easy-to-Read Version

## FAMILY

GOD CREATED THE FAMILY UNIT TO be relational. Your family begins with you and your spouse. If you are blessed with children, then your family simply expands from two members to three and so on. Embracing that parenting is one of the highest callings we could ever partner with God on; that is when we can receive one of the richest blessings ever to be experienced. We actually are given the honor of partnering with God to shape and mold another human life that He has ordained for a specific work in our world. WOW! What an honor and privilege. Why would we let anything distract us from such a responsibility? Work, the to-do list, overcommitments—they can all steal time from a top priority in your life—your family. This is true whether you are married or single, have children or not.

In his book *The Little Red Book of Wisdom*, Mark DeMoss reflects, "What defines us is not one large intention to be a good person, or parent—it's 100,000 ongoing choices of every size that arise when we are tired, satisfied, distracted, full of ourselves, threatened, happy, reactionary, sentimental, hurried, bored.... We're talking about every person's option, sooner or later, to live deliberately."

There is nothing worse than living life with regrets. I don't want that for my life. Honestly, I don't think anybody wants that. However, we seem to find ourselves in that situation from time to time. There's something about society's hold on us, our busyness, our drive to do great things, and the expectations that are forced upon us that can steal away moments of our lives. Energy is put into "important efforts," and our actions indicate that our family is what we do on the side when we are not busy at work. This goes for men and women. Starting now, starting today, this very minute, you can experience inexpressible joy simply by making a decision to place a value on things that matter most.

Many people may look at my life and think that it is easy for me to be filled with joy because my life seems so perfect. I promise you, nobody's life is perfect. I have experienced traumatic things in my life that no child or adult should ever have to go through. There are countless situations that could have destroyed me, my marriage, and my family. Times were hard, situations were rough, and I didn't always respond well. Actually, I think my first response usually was anger. But in the long run, what was going to drive me? Joy. It's joy that gives us freedom in difficult times. It's our choices that can make life bitter (a victim mentality) or sweeter (an overcomer mentality). Which one sounds more hopeful to you?

We have a choice to make in every aspect of our lives. It's funny to think about this, but the average person makes anywhere from thirty-five thousand to fifty thousand conscious and unconscious choices a day. Make your choices matter. You are worth the effort. Your family is worth the effort. What life could be, the experiences you share, are priceless treasures waiting for you to discover.

As Frances Knott George shared in another Facebook post:

> Treasure your time at home with your children. No one loves your children as much as you. No regrets. Mistakes along the way in parenting? Certainly. But no regrets in giving up' all the world says is so important for the privilege of being Mom. [I'm] grateful to have had the time to raise my treasures and then give them wings.

## FRIENDS AND RELATIONSHIPS

I would also love to encourage you to invest time into other relationships. I promise you; there is nothing more fulfilling, more precious, or more special than relationships with others. When we fight the opportunity to build relationships, we miss out on incredible joys of life. I have learned this firsthand.

I mentioned previously that we were able to spend a year in Austin, Texas. This is an incredible testimony as to the lengths the Lord had to go to grab my attention. I was living a very comfortable, secluded life. We visited Austin in November 2012 for a business event. We never thought for one moment that we would be living there. One morning I awoke, and as soon as my eyes popped open, even before Dale was awake, I turned over, shook him on the shoulder and said, "You know what we should do today? Look at apartments, just for the fun of it."

Still we had no intentions to move. Once we arrived back home in North Carolina, I had a gnawing in my soul that I needed to be back in Austin. This quickly turned into a feeling of physical pain and even panic. After a week, I finally shared my pain with Dale, and he responded, "I feel the same way." I almost passed out—literally! I must have gasped so loud that the sucking in of air almost knocked me out.

You see, Dale has lived within the same ten-mile radius his whole life. He has NEVER wanted to move—ever! We knew that God was directing us to take this adventure. I said to my husband, "I know that God wants us to go to Austin, Texas, so that I can help people get healthy." It made sense. That's what we do for a living. I was sure that's how He was going to use me in Texas. We were very excited, full of hope and anticipation about how God was going to move in our business.

Once we got to Texas in January 2013, we started digging in to find people to meet. Both Dale and I joined networking events, met people in our community, and spent every weekend attending three to four different church services. It was crazy! We were having fun, but our goal was to meet people that we were supposed to help get healthy. By March, I was completely and entirely burned out. I had no joy, was stressed out and tired, and had no clients to show for all our efforts.

I heard about a women's Bible study at one of the churches and became extremely excited to participate. I knew that this was meant for me. You see, I had done this particular study before in Raleigh. It was through Beth Moore's book *David, A Man After God's Own Heart*. I felt I could "slide through" the course without having to do any work. I even called my daughter back home and had her mail my workbook to me. I could be there simply to meet people whom I was supposed to help get healthy. It is so funny how God works. Little did I know, but He didn't care why *I* thought I was there. He just wanted me there.

During this Bible study, I had another one of those catalyst moments. One week we were studying how Jesus related to people. In the workbook for that particular week, there were five circles. Each circle had a number that represented a different demographic. Moore talked about how Jesus related to the world, to the seventy-two disciples, to the twelve apostles, to His three closest friends, and then to God. What really struck me like an arrow between the eyes was how Moore described Jesus's relationship with His three closest friends and confidants: Peter, James, and John. She goes on to explain that we, women in particular, have our "BFFs," our closest friends. I felt very confident for a moment. "I have my three," I thought to myself; one is in Atlanta, one in Raleigh, and one in Asheville.

As we looked closer at Jesus's relationship with the three, they walked with Him and were physically present with Him. Moore wrote about how important it is for us to have those close relationships with people who see us eyeball-to-eyeball, walk the line with us, hold us accountable, know when we're doing what we're supposed to, and know when we stray a little off course. Our closest friends could not be in different countries, states, or cities. They had to be eyeball-to-eyeball with us on a daily basis to "do life" with us.

My world was crushed at that particular moment. You see, my safe place is on stage. As I mentioned earlier, in college I majored in flute performance. When I was on stage in front of five thousand people, it didn't faze me, not one bit. I was willing to talk about things that I couldn't even spell. It didn't matter. I felt bulletproof on that stage. I used to say, "The minute I walk out of my house, I'm onstage." Why? Because I didn't have to get to know anyone. I could keep people at a safe distance and be very superficial.

I'm a black-and-white-type person. I don't live in the gray, and I don't like the gray, and I believe that every gray situation can be broken down into a black or white aspect. Relationships are messy. They take time, energy, thought, compassion—all things I didn't want to give. I could walk into a room of three hundred people and call them all friends. But how many people did I do life with? Not a single one!

I had made a very comfortable, safe cocoon for myself in my home. Many people would swear that I am an extrovert, but really, I am an introvert. I rejuvenate being totally alone. I lived in the same small town outside of Raleigh for eighteen years and personally knew six people in that town. Our whole lives were lived in Raleigh, and we just slept in our tiny town. I didn't want to take the effort to get messy and really know people, their life stories, their deepest hurts, and their greatest joys. It was easier to keep my distance. Comfortable. That is not the best way to live, especially when God has big plans for you to grow.

As I pieced together the realization from the Bible study, I battled with God for weeks on this subject, and it got ugly. I would yell, out loud, "I did not come to Texas to build relationships! I came here to get people healthy and build my business!" If you have ever fought with God, you know it is exhausting. It was a very dark and depressing month in my life. I even had a friend look at me and say, "When you walk into a room your countenance is not very welcoming. The stress is all over you." Great! I was so frustrated. How could He bring me to Texas for relationships? After all, I didn't have those types of relations back home in my community; why would I seek them here? That was not my forte. My specialty was performing—including being great at a false front.

Please allow me to stop for a moment. I have to say, even as I typed that paragraph, I had tears in my eyes because of what the Lord has done in my life. I'm so grateful for His mercy, guidance, and softening of my heart. Most of all, I am in a place of gratitude for the beautiful friendships He allowed me to discover, nurture, and cherish.

After I stopped fighting with God, I made it a point to get to know people in Austin, to be relational, to care about them. The sweetest thing that came from my time in Texas was the relationships He allowed me to form with three incredibly beautiful and special women. We shared life together, mentored one other, supported one other, and most of all loved one another. Even to this day, when I go back to Austin, the first thing I do is see who's ready to get together. One of those friends is even moving to Raleigh! How's that for God orchestrating things in His perfect way?

I began to get a little scared that God was calling me to stay in Austin. We had only made a one-year commitment to be there; however, was I wrong about that too? I'm thankful that He made it very clear that I was not supposed to start over in Austin. During the year we were in Texas, my daughter Kim became engaged, got married, instantly inherited a sweet one-year-old son, and got pregnant with her first baby. Our son also became engaged that year! It was certainly time to come home. I felt I needed to take the things learned and implement them within my existing relationships and community. I had a few friends to reconnect with and several relationships to repair. I had been oblivious to the fact that I had hurt people. God helped me to restore a few of those relationships.

When we returned home, that is exactly what I did. Knowing six people in my town was not good enough anymore. I quickly became involved with my local chamber of commerce and two other chambers within a fifteen-mile radius of my house. I became a Rotarian in our community and even sit on the board of directors for our local Boys & Girls Club. I connected with other homeschool moms, volunteered with local church and community events, and looked for ways to be of value in service to the people around me.

I think it's safe to say that now I know no stranger. I love to meet people. Everywhere I go, whether it's to shop at a store thirty minutes away or take a trip cross-country, wherever I am, I am looking to find friends. I use Facebook as a wonderful way to connect. I love adding at least ten new friends on Facebook every single day. I want to use that social media platform as a way to build relationships, to inspire, to encourage, to give hope, and to be a light in people's lives. It doesn't take long to send somebody a private message to show you care. I, very humbly, desire to share with you a post from my friend Patricia Wells that brought tears to my eyes. This is a huge testimony to the work that God is doing in my life and how he is allowing me to see that I am transforming into the person he desires me to become. Joyful living is not something you do; it is who you become.

> I want to take a moment to say thank you to Honey Beth Wiggs. She doesn't know this, but she has been a rock for me during a very tough transition these past few months and seeing her today made me realize just how much of an impact she was. We don't talk everyday, not even every week, but she has not forgotten about me during her busy life. She takes time out for me, asks me how I am, checks in on me, lets me vent, get out my frustrations and, with very little effort, she encourages me to find the positive in everything. No matter how small that positive is, she has shown me that it is there. Today I was lucky enough to hug her and hear her say, 'See, God laid it all out.' At this moment, that brings tears to my eyes because of how true it

> is. I still have healing to do, but having you on my side Honey Beth Wiggs is a wonderful feeling. Thank you for being you! Thank you for your sincerity! Thank you for helping me! Thank you for everything!!

Where do you start building these types of relationships? Start with your family. If they are close by, have a big meal together once a week. Remember I mentioned how Dale's mom always cooked on the weekends? Those were the best times for our family. My older kids have so many fond memories of those nights, sitting outside by the fire, talking for hours. Make family time a priority, no matter how big or small.

Find organizations that you can support with time or donations and get to know the people. Look for ways to be of service and value that fit your stage in life, area of expertise, and joy! Make a decision and start. Anywhere. Baby steps. Just start.

Are you beginning to see a pattern? It starts with practicing the art of dreaming, getting a clear vision of what you desire for you and your family (which is one of your top priorities), then implementing a plan of action while surrounding yourself with like-minded people who you are meeting and building relationships with. What a sweet, joy filled life you can experience and create, especially when you have the freedom to live life to the fullest—the topic of our next chapter.

# 7 Freedom

> "For I know the plans I have for you," declares the Lord, "
> ...plans to give you hope and a future."
> Jeremiah 29:11, New International Version

WHEN YOU CAN FORGE A NEW path down uncharted territory, you open the doors to experience the sweet surprises of joy around every bend in the road. I am a firm believer that it is important to be ready to do the things we are being called to do—to accomplish in our lives. There are three aspects of freedom that need to be in place in order to have total freedom: time, finances, and expectations. If we had not had "our house in order"—meaning our time, freedom, and finances in order—we would not have been ready to pick up and move to Texas within a few weeks of hearing that call on our lives.

## TIME

Having the time to be of service and value to others, to serve as a family when others can't, is a beautiful thought to me. What a blessing to have the freedom to pick up at a moment's notice and drive someone to a doctor appointment, go grocery shopping in the middle of the day for an elderly family member, or go on a mission trip in the middle of a school year? This is what we desire, to create something so beautiful that would allow us the time to pay it forward and be a sweet blessing to others.

Would you agree that many wonderful experiences would happen for you and your family if you had the freedom of time? I do. Our family vision was to travel as much as possible before the kids got into high school. I knew that I wanted to create experiences for my children, but trying to cram a year's worth of life into a short summer break from school was not going to fit our plan. I decided that in order for us to have the life we desired, I needed to homeschool, and I've been doing it ever since. Every year I consider my options, but we always seem to choose to homeschool. The reason is simple. I love the freedom of time it allows our family. We can pick up at any given moment and head off on a great adventure for a few hours, a day, a week, or a month. Total time freedom with our family is what we desired for our lives.

Now, I might have just frightened some of you with the concept of homeschooling your children to create time, but it is OK! As I said, I don't necessarily like homeschooling, but I do absolutely *love* the freedom homeschooling gives to our family for travel. Remember, stay open to new ideas. This may or may not be an option for you, and that is perfectly fine. This is your life, your journey, your choices. My desire is for you to see how you can make decisions to center your life around what matters most.

Time is precious. We only have a few short years with our children under our wings before they start to spread their own wings and soar. What are the dreams you envisioned and wrote down in the beginning of this book? What do you want to bring to reality? Do you need freedom of time to accomplish those goals? What steps can you take to create the freedom of time in your life? Are you starting to think and consider what that could look like for you? Are there areas you need to let go?

Hiring out help, in my opinion, can be one of the smartest ways to free up your time. I had an opportunity to bless someone, a person super special to me that I love dearly, who desired a new job and loved my kids. For three beautiful, wonderful, amazing years of our lives (2010–2013—oh, I will never forget them), I was able to hire my daughter Kim to be my personal assistant. She helped me in the office and homeschooled my younger kids. She even traveled with us so Dale and I could go to events together, enjoy dates with each other, and do some exploring without the kids. Talk about freeing up my time. This allowed me to focus on building my business so we could really enjoy life. And guess what? It worked!

This leads us to another aspect of our lives that needed to be in place for us to move our dreams forward. We may have had the freedom of time, but we needed the freedom of finances to take our adventures to the next level.

## FINANCES

I worked for almost twenty years at my church in Raleigh. In April 1993, I started as a part-time housekeeper. I quickly became full-time as housekeeping supervisor and over the years worked as set-up coordinator, church calendar supervisor, administrative assistant, and receptionist. My last eight years were spent serving a wonderful pastor with whom I was also blessed to lead praise music almost every Sunday. It was during this time that God was really shaping me to create health in my life. Not only was He showing me how I was ruining my body due to my unhealthy habits, but He was also awakening a heart to assist others in their health journeys.

Even though I lost a hundred pounds in order to have children, I was not healthy. Six years after giving birth to my second child, I still had a good eighty pounds to lose. The realization that I was turning into a diabetic, coupled with the conviction that my body is the dwelling place of Christ, inspired me to take action. Little did I know that the decision to create health in my life would touch over fifteen thousand lives (and counting) across America.

In August 2008, I started my personal health journey, first as a client with the program I now coach. I felt amazing! The transformation happening in my body, mind, and spirit caused a tsunami of change in every area of my life. In September 2008, just one month into my journey, I became a certified health coach in order to assist others on the same path. Talk about exhilarating. When you have the opportunity to give people hope and help for something that they have struggled with for so long, the fulfillment and joy is deep and addictive.

In January 2009, I made a decision to direct all of my energy into helping others create wonderful transformations in their lives, guiding them to optimal well-being with a healthy body, healthy mind, and healthy finances. Once I focused my energies to match my goal, in three months I was able to match what I was making at my full-time church position.

It would be great for me to tell you that I took all of that extra income and made a nice six-month emergency fund. Sadly though, financial guru Dave Ramsey would be a little disappointed in me. While we did set aside a portion, we went back to our foundational thought: Life is short. We are not promised tomorrow. So what's a girl to do?

We started living adventures, creating experiences, making memories to last a lifetime. I could begin to see our dreams come to fruition. The excitement in my soul from seeing people achieve their dreams while glimpsing a vision of mine coming true spurred me on every day. In June 2010, I retired from my church position and became a full-time certified health coach. That decision was not easy. I absolutely loved my job, but the vision of freedom, from expectations and of time, along with the vision for growing finances to fuel my life and the life of my family, was not going to come to fruition unless I stepped out in faith.

This gigantic leap into the unknown allowed me to work from home and be with my family all the time. That certainly took some adjustment on my part. When you leave a nine-to- five job, it can sometimes be difficult to find your rhythm when you are at home and your own boss. After a few months of feeling like I was on vacation, I finally found my ebb and flow. Having my daughter work for me gave me the freedom I needed to build my business. Because of those steps, in October 2012, I was able to allow my husband to retire from his construction-related business. What an amazing accomplishment that I will never take for granted. This is what I stepped out in faith to accomplish when I quit my job. We now had 100 percent freedom, time, and money to center our lives around what mattered most, just in time for God to call us to spend a year in Austin, Texas.

Plan to have fun with your life. This can even be done on a budget. I mastered this so well that in 2005 I developed a seminar titled "Partying on a Penny, Vacationing on a Dime." We joked with friends of ours all the time that we would stay at cheap hotels with free breakfast, make lunches and snacks out of the breakfast selections, then print out all the local restaurant guides to what nights kids would eat free. You can laugh, but I know some of you know exactly what I am talking about. I promise you, where there is a will, there is a way! You know it is true.

In order for you to create the finances needed to fulfill your dreams, you may need to become creative and step out in faith. Are there things you can give up for a short period of time? That cup of coffee-shop coffee every morning? Getting your weekly manicure and pedicure? Dinner out? What about taking on a small part-time job or a seasonal or holiday job for a few months? What about starting a small business? I know if you set your mind to it, you can think of many creative ways, and even new and exciting ways, to fund the adventures deep within your soul.

Being ready to move in a new direction, to serve and to give abundantly with your time and finances, is definitely one aspect of freedom. Another aspect is freeing yourself from unnecessary expectations placed on you either by yourself or by others.

## EXPECTATIONS

In my mind, expectations can be broken down into two categories: necessary and optional. We all have expectations placed upon us that take priority. A mom of young children is expected to make sure her children are fed and bathed. A full-time employee is expected to work certain hours per the hiring agreement. An older son may be expected to care of an aging parent. All of these types of situations are necessary expectations that we willingly take on.

On the flip side are optional expectations, sometimes placed on us by others, that derail our focus and energy. This is where we need to be alert, because the freedom we are working to create may slowly slip through our fingers. A mom is asked to bake cookies for a meeting and then expected to do it every week. An employee is expected to work on weekends when that wasn't part of the contract when hired. A man decides to cut a neighbor's grass as a favor and then is expected to do it every week. You fill in the blank. While tasks may seem good, if they are forced, draining you of energy, making you bitter, or taking more time than you have to give, then consider the option of freeing yourself from such unnecessary pressure. Always remember your goal, the vision for what you are creating in your life, and set clear expectations with yourself and others.

I would love to share a personal example with you of what it looked like for me when I spent time doing things out of expectations instead of joy.

I really don't like teaching at all, even though I am gifted as a teacher. It's exactly why I was a performance major, not an education major. While I was working full-time and going to school, I kept thinking about what I was going to do with my music. The voice from society kept ringing in my head saying, "You have to teach music." So, I began a short-lived career having a flute studio and teaching band at a few private Christian schools in the area. I was miserable! Absolutely, 100 percent, miserable. I had no joy. Everyone kept telling me what a great teacher I was. If I was such a great teacher, why did I hate it so much?

In one of my beautiful morning quiet times, I physically heard God say to me, "Honey Beth, I never told you to teach music to children." Oh, my word! That was one of the most freeing mornings in my life—ever! The very next day doors were opening for me to speak at adoption events, share my testimony, and later, as God would unfold my path, guide adults and families in healthy living.

When I think about optional expectations, one event stands out in my mind. One year we decided to skip all the family visits over the holidays and spend several weeks in December traveling, just the four of us: me, Dale, and our two young children. I have *a lot* of family. I have a mom and stepdad, dad and stepmom, mother-in-law, and grown stepchildren who have just as many relatives to coordinate. I am also adopted and have great relationships with my birth mother and birth father. Add them into the mix, and you can see how overwhelming holidays can be. When we announced we would be gone for three weeks with our five- and four-year-old, we got a few strange looks from friends and family.

We packed our two-foot Christmas tree in the car and spent twenty days between Orlando, Florida, and Nashville, Tennessee. Spending Christmas morning in our hotel room, going down to breakfast in jammies, and then opening presents in the room with our two-foot tree was so much fun that we have done it several times since. It was refreshing to be relaxed and away from the crazy pace and expectations of the holiday. We had no expectations of ourselves, and no one else had expectations of us.

What did we actually accomplish over the Christmas holiday? We created freedom. We set a new path for new traditions with our family. Creating freedom in several areas of your life is key to experiencing that joy filled life. I guess I am a bit of a rebel, and I love to encourage others to "buck the system." The way of "doing life" that was passed down to us for generations, from society's box, no longer is the only way to "do life." Remember, it is not about *doing* but *becoming*. Being driven by the expectations of others is a sure-fire way to lose sight of what you are creating for your joy filled life.

When I was a new mom, I was beginning to feel that my life was about to take a drastic turn, away from my hopes and dreams. I was out to prove that life does not end when you have children. It was just the beginning of a bigger and better adventure designed for me. You can create this for yourself as well. Release yourself from any guilt or fear related to placing priority on creating a life that will lead to a legacy of joy for everyone around you. Be an example and lead the way.

What are some areas of expectations that you might be thinking about in different ways? How might you create an environment or clarity of expectations so that you can live according to your hopes and dreams, your true desires? How can you think outside the box and forge a new path by adjusting expectations? It may take time to begin the shift, but I believe you will find it rewarding.

I took a leap of faith into unchartered territory for our family by freeing us from expectations as well as freeing up time. The results are super sweet. Every day we have a blank canvas to create anything we desire. What are you realizing that you could design if you had the time, finances, and freedom from expectations to create the joy filled life you desire?

# HOW TO DO IT

Up to this time you have not asked a single thing in my name, but now ask and keep on asking and you will receive, so that your joy may be full and complete.
John 16:24, New English Translation

AS OUR JOURNEY TOGETHER BEGINS TO wind down, I hope you have started to dream about the life you wish to create and realize the value of placing priority on your family unit. You should now have a pretty clear idea of what you want to create in your life and family. Keep asking the question "What if?" in order to allow your heart's desires to surface. A portion of people spend more time dreaming about their future than living it. One of the sweetest ways to grow memories is to schedule adventures. Treasured moments and memorable experiences for your family can happen in a few hours, a day, a week, or longer. The length doesn't matter—only that the adventures happen. Let's look at how we can do it.

# 8

# A Lean Lifestyle

> Lord, you give me all that I need. You support me.
> You give me my share.
> Psalms 16:5, Easy-to-Read Version

AS YOU MAY HAVE NOTICED IN the previous chapters, you don't need material possessions to have a happy heart and cheerful mind. Both of those gifts come from centering yourself in a place of gratitude, care, and rest while enjoying the relationships you have been given. Almost every day I get messages from people thanking me for always being a positive influence on social media and texts of appreciation for uplifting encouragement. At least once a week, I am asked the question "How do you manage to live such a joyful and exciting life?" Or I receive comments such as "You are so lucky" and "I wish I could live your life." I am nobody special. You are no different from me. I am not lucky, and karma has nothing to do with it. I simply made a decision on how I wanted to live life, got clear on my vision, charted out a plan, and took action. I promise you, it is not always easy or pretty, but it *is* simple. Sometimes there are hard decisions to make, and that is when I keep private things private and choose joy in the hard times.

Whether in health, mind-set, or relationships, I am constantly choosing to act and respond in ways that represent my goals and me. I only have control over one single person, and that is me. What I do, how I do it, and how it affects others is totally up to me. I am the composer of my beautiful symphony called "life." That's why it's so important to be crystal clear on your vision, your family mission statement. If there are decisions to make, and they do not line up with your mission, then you have to choose between what you want now and what you want most. And that goes for every single area of your life.

I had to make some hard choices in my life. For example, when I made the decision to leave my job of almost twenty years. I had thoroughly loved my position with Pastor Joel Leath and had looked forward to working with my friend every day. It had been a fulfilling job, but for me to move forward to the next level of a fulfilled life, I knew I had to step out in faith. How was I able to do that? By making smaller daily decisions that helped our family live a leaner lifestyle.

For several years we chose to live a very simple and modest lifestyle. As you would travel from the big city of Raleigh east, into the country, you pulled into our tiny town and enjoyed some beautiful country back roads. The moment you turned into our bumpy gravel driveway, you would see our humble home, which we purchased when we first got married. Our house was not fancy, nor did it have all of the latest gadgets, appliances, or furniture.

Probably the number one thing somebody would notice when they entered our home would be the lack of televisions. That's right—no TV at all. We made a decision many years ago to get rid of TV. There were several reasons. I was paying almost a hundred dollars a month for a plethora of channels, only to have five unlocked for viewing. Also, I could not get my kids to do their schoolwork because they always wanted to watch TV. So we took care of that problem in a flash, along with getting rid of our Xbox and PlayStation. The two greatest aspects about this decision were that I saved a hundred dollars a month, and it allowed us to have more quality family time in the evening. We began playing cards and board games, putting puzzles together, and having family devotionals before bed.

The other thing we realized, a blessing really, is that when we were not distracted by the television, we had more time to do the things that we desired to do in order to make our dreams and vision a reality. It is amazing how much time gets sucked up in front of the "boob tube," as my older relatives used to say. Getting rid of the TV allowed us to save money and expand our time, almost exponentially, which in turn allowed me to grow my business.

A house is just a house unless you make it a home. Our house was filled with love, joy, fun, and memories. And in reality, it was just a place for us to lay our heads and do laundry until the next adventure. Could we have purchased a large, beautiful home in the country or in the city? Absolutely. But for that particular season of life, staying in our home with a super tiny mortgage payment made more sense. It allowed us to enjoy wonderful destinations while staying at five-star resorts and enjoying gourmet meals. It helped make the season of life with our teenagers super enjoyable.

Another thing that we did for many years was avoid purchasing new vehicles. We love to drive. Not only is it a fun way to see the country, but mileage is also a fantastic tax deduction for my business. One of my cars had been cross-country several times, with over 350,000 miles on the odometer. Many things went bad, such as starters, batteries, tires, engines, and transmissions. Thinking practically, and wanting to save money, when parts broke, we chose to fix them rather than purchase a new car. At the time, a new transmission was much cheaper than a new car. We had no car payments and liked it that way. Now this does not mean we never bought a new car, but getting lean for a short period of time allowed us to store away money so that when we did eventually purchase new vehicles or a new house, we could pay cash and avoid debt.

There are many other ways that you can get lean with your lifestyle and finances. These are just some of the things we chose to do. Maybe it has inspired you to look at your life and see where you might be able to get lean for a short period of time. Take a few minutes to think about areas in your life where you can begin to "get lean" in order to help finance joyful adventures, and make a list of them below.

________________________________________

________________________________________

________________________________________

________________________________________

________________________________________

________________________________________

________________________________________

________________________________________

________________________________________

________________________________________

To start enjoying family adventures, it takes more vision than resources. As I've said before, you have to start dreaming and make a plan.

You can find creative ways to finance your adventures. Where there is a will, there's always a way. You might simplify your lifestyle, hold a yard sale, host a bake sale, create a lemonade stand, save your change, have the kids save a portion of their earned money, put aside a certain percentage from each paycheck into a special savings account, suggest donations to an adventure for birthdays and holidays, or do what I did, start your own business being of service and value to others. Whatever your choices, there is always a way to find the resources needed to fund the next great family adventure. Those decisions I made years ago have led me to a path of an extremely successful home-based career that allows me to live a much sweeter life.

Remember, never judge a book by its cover. Just because someone has all the latest gadgets and toys doesn't mean that person has time and freedom to enjoy life. Creating a happy heart and cultivating a joyful mind can leave you in such a glorious state of well-being that you will enjoy looking for ways to live lean for a short period of time in order to have a beautiful, sweet future.

# 9 Implementing Adventure

Be very careful, then, how you live—not as unwise but as wise, making the most of every opportunity...
Ephesians 5:15–16a, New International Versiona

## EXPLORE YOUR COMMUNITY/CITY

THIS IS ONE OF THE EASIEST ways to start having adventures with your family. I grew up in Maryland, right outside of Washington, DC. As a kid, I spent a lot of time downtown on the Mall. I have great memories of that. I know several people who have lived in the DC area for years and never explored the Washington Monument. It's funny to me. When we go on vacations, sometimes we know more about what there is to do in the city than some locals.

Many people have lived in their city for years and have never explored it like a tourist. I would encourage you to do that. Take a weekend, stay in a hotel downtown if you can, and pretend you are visiting. Enjoy going to new places, seeing new things, even talking to people from different states. It can be so much fun. Take a trolley tour, go on a walking history tour, pick up all of the flyers in the information kiosk next to the front desk of a hotel, or eat at a new restaurant. You will be surprised with all the new treasures you find.

If you embrace social media, I suggest that you look for Facebook community pages. I live in a tiny town. I was floored to find ten local community pages that I could join, including town and chamber of commerce pages. In my opinion, the chamber of commerce is the most underutilized organization by community members. The first thing I would suggest is to check with your local chamber for advice on restaurants, parks, entertainment, and unique things to do. You would be amazed at how many fabulous locations you may not even know about. The chamber's website is where all of the news is shared about upcoming events for the community. Start joining those social media pages and looking at them consistently.

Another great idea is to put a few apps on your phone. I highly suggest LivingSocial, Groupon, and RetailMeNot. These websites will give you ideas, deals, and coupons for things to do locally, not only in your hometown but also any city you visit. It is a whole lot of fun to take a trip knowing that you already have an itinerary planned that cost you very little time and money.

### DAY TRIPS WITHIN YOUR STATE

Have you made it a point to explore your state? Go to your favorite library or bookstore and look for books on things to do in your state (or any other state). You can find free activities, low-cost activities, and full-out adventures to enjoy. Another idea is to ask people on those local Facebook pages about certain destinations within your state. Ask people for their favorite place to visit. It is fun to connect with other like-minded people and to encourage one another to live a joy filled life centered around what matters most. And guess what? There are probably Facebook group pages for those specific destination areas. These are pages where people can share experiences, photos, and ideas for enjoying that city. It also gives you great opportunities to build relationships.

My great friend "Aunt Josie"—as my kids call her—lives in a different state. I have gone to her house and enjoyed several day trips exploring her own backyard. It is fun to simply drive and "get lost" every now and then. Sometimes that is when you find the most wonderful surprises. Where can you explore that might be right around the corner?

**SHORT TRIPS**

Another option, which we took advantage of for several years, was to take several three- or four-day weekends. I remember one year, early in our marriage, I was working full-time and had ten vacation days. By using holidays, I was able to arrange seven four- to five-day weekends away with my family. I used those adventure getaways to fuel my focus at work. I kept working hard to get to the next adventure—filling the spaces of time. It's amazing how exciting and motivating anticipation of something wonderful can be.

Josie and I started taking little three- to five-day getaways together. Occasionally we would fly to a destination and spend a few days there or drive and meet each other somewhere. Oh, the stories that we could tell! To this day, we still go away together at least once, if not twice, a year.

Think about what your family can do to make the most out of vacation days or school breaks. You can even make this subject that focus of family meals or of time in the car driving to and from appointments. It allows you to dream as a family as well, and that is when momentum toward a joy filled life really gets going!

## EXTENDED FAMILY/FRIEND VISITS

Do you have friends or family who live out of town? That is a great way to explore and experience different areas without having to spend a lot of money. Once I moved to the Raleigh area, most of my family and friends were still back home in Maryland. In the early years of our marriage, we would hop in the car and go stay with friends and family in Maryland in order to take the kids on tours of Washington, DC.

I would love to share something fun with you. Every time we have a close friend tell us of a planned move, we get so excited. That becomes another place for us to visit where we will have a connection. It has opened the whole United States to us!

We had friends that moved from Raleigh to Moses Lake, Washington. This is a small "desert oasis" town between Seattle and Spokane. I sang with these friends on a praise team at church. We both had young kids the same ages. While they were in Raleigh, we went to their house one time. Once! When they moved out to Washington, we flew out there four times to visit them. We would fly into Seattle; take the kids up the Space Needle; stop at Pike Place Market and pick up lobster tails, shrimp, and flowers; and then drive two and a half hours over the mountains into the desert. Those were such great adventures and memories. On one trip, we even took more friends with us.

Here is another example. Remember I mentioned earlier that we spent one December in Hawaii? Guess what? We had a friend who lived in Oahu because her husband was in the military. I shared with her that my daughter had started a dog-sitting service. She happened to have a dog that needed sitting over the Christmas holiday. Well, how could we not help a friend out? To make it even more interesting, one of our neighbors from Texas was going away for the New Year's holiday of that same year. Who else to call other than the "Wiggs Traveling Dog Sitters" to stay for ten days in Austin? We were gone a month, enjoying life, family, and friends—all while making memories to last a lifetime.

Do you have a family member who lives in a different state that you haven't seen in a while? When was the last time you visited your old college roommate or high school friends? Think about where you might have some connections, and see if you can start to plan a little trip to reconnect and make lasting memories.

## SMART SAVINGS

In 2007, because of our flexible schedule, we were able to travel the equivalent of seven months out of the entire year. Some of those trips were cruises, but a lot of that time was spent in hotel rooms. How did we afford it? I was so skilled at bidding on hotel rooms and rental cars on Priceline that I started giving seminars on it. There are many ways now, with the advancement of technology, that you can economically travel. Searching Google for discount hotels, flights, entertainment, and food will bring up pages of wonderful websites to visit. I also suggest using Instagram, Facebook, and Pinterest to search for and follow people who have visited, blogged about, lived in, or frequently traveled to your destination.

Another fantastic resource is the chamber of commerce in the destination city you plan to explore, as I hinted earlier. The chamber knows all the great deals and hidden gems within its city. Plus, it is there to build revenue within its city, so its members are going to be more than happy to assist you. Shop local, folks!

Another way to save money and guarantee an adventure is to vacation with friends. To rent an oceanfront house at the beach for a week could cost an arm and a leg. If you were to split the cost between two other families, all of a sudden it would become an affordable vacation that would be bound to be memorable.

### HOTEL REWARDS AND FREQUENT FLYER MILES

Over the past years, I have found the value and benefits of hotel and airline rewards to be amazing for our family. I have two credit cards that I use for travel: Marriott and American Airlines. While I fly airlines other than American, I must say, I have become a Marriott junkie. I mean that sincerely. We stay at nothing but Marriott hotels. I've done a lot of research, and I truly believe that Marriott has the best rewards program around. Not only do you get the most benefits for the points you earn, but you also have access to a fabulous concierge lounge that serves breakfast, snacks, and drinks throughout the day along with a light dinner five days a week! Even with all those perks, what I most enjoy is the customer service. I love nothing better than to pick up the phone every morning and hear, "Good morning, Mrs. Wiggs. How can we help you today?" Who wouldn't love that?

My suggestion to you is to find a hotel chain that you enjoy and become a loyal customer. There are benefits that will help you receive the most bang for your buck. You may also find that certain destinations may open up to you that you never considered before, simply because that hotel brand was represented somewhere you never imagined going.

If you plan on flying a lot, I suggest you get an airline credit card. Again, those points can add up fast, and frequent flyer miles are great things to have, not only for you but also for others as well. You receive access to many benefits, including lounges, shorter lines, faster boarding, and sometimes free seating upgrades.

A wonderful benefit of having hotel discounts or credits and airline miles is that when people are in need or you want to bless someone, you can use those as a gift to bring joy to someone else's life. We have done that many times, with family, friends and people in need, and it is a great honor to be a blessing to someone else.

## CRUISES

Early in our marriage we loved to cruise. For a family of four, we found it was an economical vacation. All of your food, gratuities, and onboard entertainment are included in the price. Traveling to a port of call doesn't have to be difficult, considering cruises leave from almost anywhere with water. Some people have opinions about certain cruise lines being better than others, and that may be true. I believe for the most part that any cruise line's three- to five-day cruises are party boats, whereas the seven- to ten-day cruises tend to be more family oriented.

The first cruise we took with our children was extremely memorable. My son was twenty-two months old, and my daughter was nine months old. Packing for a weeklong cruise with two little ones is no easy feat. I had one suitcase for diapers, one for toys, one for the kids' formula and food, and two for all of our clothing. When we added a Pack 'n Play to the mix, Dale and I felt like mules. It was hilarious. I had a kid on each hip and diaper bags strapped around my arms while Dale attempted to carry all the suitcases.

My biggest fear was that my son would jump off the side of the ship. I quickly became one of those moms. You know, the moms that say, "Oh, I will never do that," but when they have children, immediately do it? I am referring to the baby leash. We bought three baby leashes: two for my son and one for my daughter. She usually hung from my chest, just in case she wiggled out of her harness.

Have you ever considered going on a cruise? Is that something you would love to do? Start looking at destinations and ports of call and book it! Usually you only need to provide a deposit and pay the rest later or in installments. I suggest that once it is booked, look for a Facebook group page for that particular cruise (nine times out of ten there is one) and start getting to know some of the other families that will be on the ship. This is yet another great way to build new relationships.

### THEME PARKS

Do you remember my story about being kicked off a roller coaster? Not anymore. I love riding roller coasters and enjoying that type of excitement and adrenaline with my family. One way to ensure that you enjoy theme parks is to purchase season passes to the park nearest you.

We are platinum pass holders for Busch Gardens. These passes allow us to get into any Sea World or Busch Gardens theme or water park across the United States. And we have been to every single one, several times. Because of the passes, we get special seating at many shows within the parks. No waiting in lines. There are other theme parks that do the same thing, so just look for the nearest one to you and inquire. You might even be able to find extra savings for being a local resident.

### PARKS/MUSEUMS

Season passes can be found for almost any type of park. The National Park Service has America the Beautiful Passes that allow you to enter any federally operated park across the country. Zoos and museums have something similar as well. Start doing research on places you might like to go, or visit often, and see what type of offers they have for other areas around the country. We are season pass holders to the Biltmore Estate in Asheville, North Carolina. Children seventeen and under get in for free. It is worth our investment to purchase passes every year in order to have hundreds of beautiful acres within which to walk, hike, canoe, horseback, tour, and shop. Sometimes we will visit and just go sit by the river and relax.

Begin to explore the many options of parks, famous landmarks, and historical battlegrounds. You may discover a growing list of exciting places to tour.

## CAMPING

Some people love it; some people don't. There are different ways to camp, including by tent, yurt, and RV. Campgrounds are extremely family friendly. You have an instant bond with your neighbors. The smells of bacon cooking on the grills for breakfast, coffee brewing, campfires at night, fresh air—there really isn't anything quite as refreshing and relaxing.

One year Dale and I went off alone for Thanksgiving while our older children were with their mom. We packed the RV and headed to Asheville. On Thanksgiving Day, I cooked a gigantic turkey in our tiny oven. I basted it with herbs, butter, and our secret ingredient, a bottle of Biltmore Wine. To this day, we still think that was the best Thanksgiving turkey ever. Wonder why? Whether in a tent or camper, exploring the nation on the ground can be very fulfilling.

I hope this chapter has given you some ideas for how to implement adventure in your own life. In fact, I hope that as you reach the end of our time together, you are bursting with ideas. Are you? Good. Now let's take you through the last step: creating your action plan.

# Part Five

## WHAT NOW

You will show me the path of life; in Your presence is fullness of joy, at Your right hand there are pleasures forevermore.
Psalms 16:11, Amplified Bible Classic Editiona

IT BRINGS ME DEEP PLEASURE TO share how the sweetness of a life well lived can bring fullness of joy. My heart's desire is to awaken and empower you to live a beautiful life, overflowing with treasured moments and no regrets. I long for you to dream, dream big and often. I wish for you to see how you can implement changes in your life to create freedom that will inspire and renew your soul for a glorious future. Now commit to your dreams and create your action plan.

# 10 Action Plan

...and your enthusiasm has stirred most of them to action.
2 Corinthians 9:2, New International Version

ARE YOU READY TO GET INTO action? What did you dream about? What excites you about moving forward? What are you looking forward to accomplishing? What needs to happen to make those dreams a reality? Do you feel overwhelmed about organizing all of those items? I can help you with that.

Below is a chart to help you plot out your joy filled experiences of life. It is time! I suggest having handy your computer, iPad, or smartphone to search the Internet to find answers to some of these questions. The more you can find out and list, the better. Remember, it may not be a trip that fills your dreams; it may be a personal accomplishment (a master's degree, new profession, new house, different car, more children, etc). Let's do this!

| STEP | DESCRIPTION |
|---|---|
| Dream Date-When | Where are you going to do your dream casting? |
| | |
| Things to Start Doing | Get healthy, self-care, relationships, family meals |
| | |
| | |
| | |
| | |
| | |
| Things to Stop Doing | Electronics over family, stress, optional expectations |
| | |
| | |
| | |
| | |
| | |
| Things to Adjust | Hiring help (sitter/assistant), overtime for a few months |
| | |
| | |
| | |
| | |
| Things to Accomplish | Education, new car, more children, new job |
| | |
| | |
| | |
| | |

| STEP | DESCRIPTION |
| --- | --- |
| Where to Travel | Places, people, how you're getting there, etc. |
| | |
| | |
| | |
| | |
| | |
| Cost | Start looking for tickets now, things to do, etc. |
| | |
| | |
| | |
| | |
| | |
| Financing | List creative ways to pay for the adventure |
| | |
| | |
| | |
| | |
| | |
| Desired Outcome | What do you envision the result of these plans to be? |
| | |
| | |
| | |
| Calendar | Get it out and *write down* the plans for the new year! |

I love this quote from Joyce Meyer: "Regret of the past and dread of the future are both 'thieves of joy.' There's only one thing that can be done about the past, and that is forget it....regret steals now!" What are you going to do now? How are you going to create the life you desire and leave a legacy of joy for generations to come?

There is so much fun in this journey. Embrace it. Allow yourself to dream without constraints. See what is deep within your soul that wells up and comes to fruition. Creating a life centered around what matters most to you is one of the most amazing and rewarding accomplishments you could ever achieve.

### LIFE IS SWEETER

Growing up, I loved music. I would listen and sing to Olivia Newton John records, and I wanted to be a star like Cher, a professional flutist, a saxophonist in a jazz band, a radio DJ, and the list goes on. I even majored in flute performance with hopes of being a part of the North Carolina Symphony or the Boston Pops Orchestra. As a child and young adult, I would share my aspirations and dreams with my mom. She always said, "I gave you the name. It's up to you to do something with it!"

Honey. The name comes from my Czechoslovakian great-grandmother's maiden name, Hunaczech. Honey. It is also one of the purest forms of sweetener we have in our world today. And the neat thing is there are so many different types. Bees that feed on specific plants render honey with unique flavors. There is blackberry, blueberry, eucalyptus, clover, heather, orange blossom, wildflower, and more. What type of honey will you use to make your life sweeter? What dreams, vision, plans, experiences, and joy will you be adding to your life? After all, everything is always sweeter with honey.

*I pray that out of his glorious riches he may strengthen you with power through his Spirit in your inner being, so that Christ may dwell in your hearts through faith. And I pray that you, being rooted and established in love, may have power, together with all the Lord's holy people, to grasp how wide and long and high and deep is the love of Christ, and to know this love that surpasses knowledge—that you may be filled to the measure of all the fullness of God. Now to him who is able to do immeasurably more than all we ask or imagine, according to his power that is at work within us, to him be the glory in the church and in Christ Jesus throughout all generations, forever and ever! Amen.*

*Ephesians 3:16–21, New International Version*

# Acknowledgments

I AM GRATEFUL FOR THE OPPORTUNITY to share this gift of joy with you. There are many people I would like to thank for their encouragement and support; however, before I do that, I need to thank God for His direction in this project. The Lord has been composing this story within my soul for years. In the summer of 2016, the book was bubbling over in my mind and I was able to easily let it flow from my soul to written word. I know with certainty that He gave me this story to share. I am grateful for the treasured moments He has allowed me to experience over the years and the ability to encourage others to live a joy filled life.

To my husband Dale, the words, "thank you" seem too small to describe how much your support means to me. Thank you for letting me get away, by myself, for three weeks to write this book. Thank you for taking care of the kids, the house, meals, etc. Thank you for being my sounding board, for bearing my burdens and letting me cry when needed. Thank you for loving me beyond words. I am forever grateful.

To my mom, Carol Reuter, you have always been my biggest cheerleader. You raised me to believe that I can do anything I decide to do. Thank you for supporting me in my good and bad decisions.

Your unfailing love has molded me into the woman, wife, mother and friend I am today. Your legacy will live on in me. I love you.

Josie Rudd, I don't know what to say other than I am glad Kenny married you. You are an amazing friend. I am grateful that the Lord allowed us to walk similar paths of life together. Our kids will remember so many wonderful experiences because of the decisions we made, especially the spur of the moment ones. You are an amazing woman and inspire me to be the best I can be every day.

Lana Batishev, thank you for encouraging me to write down the stories of my life. Without your encouragement, I may not have taken this leap of faith. I am grateful to have you in my life for so many reasons!

Kimberly Alexander, thank you for believing in my vision. I am grateful for your friendship and mentorship. This book would not have happened without your professional expertise.

Polly Letofsky, Alexandra O'Connell and Andrea Costantine, thank you for your wonderful assistance with planning, editing and interior design of this book. You are a wonderful team and I am grateful to all of you.

Berklee Wolaver, the cover of my book is amazing! Your artistic talents are phenomenal. You turned my scattered thoughts into exactly what I wanted! Thank you.

# About the Author

HONEY BETH WIGGS GREW UP IN Maryland, outside of Washington, DC. She met her husband in North Carolina and has called the Raleigh area home since 1991. Honey Beth studied flute performance at Meredith College in Raleigh as a continuing education student, worked at Providence Baptist Church for 18 years as an administrative assistant, taught band at North Raleigh Christian Academy and was a booking agent for the Annie Moses Band, based out of Nashville, TN. Honey Beth considers it a blessing to assist with the bands annual Fine Arts Summer Academy and in July of 2015 she performed with the Annie Moses Band for a PBS Special taped at the Grand Ole Opry.

Honey Beth used to struggle with her health. At one point in time she weighed 320 pounds. She tried for 10 years to have children and finally was told by a doctor, "You are too fat to have a baby!" Honey Beth found a wonderful optimal health program that allowed her to reclaim her health, have energy and center her life around wat matters most, creating a joy filled life. Not only was she able to have two beautiful children, but also find a new career path.

Honey Beth Wiggs is a bestselling author, speaker and certified health coach. Since 2008, her coaching practice has been able to assist over 15,000 people to create long term well-being. She serves on the board for local chambers of commerce and community programs. Honey Beth is an accomplished flutist, who still performs, and loves to sing. She currently lives outside of Raleigh, NC with her husband Dale and two teenage children. She also has two older children and 5 grandchildren. Honey Beth homeschools her children in order to create freedom to travel and make memorable lifelong experiences with her family. She has a passion for living life to the fullest and inspires others to do the same. Honey Beth desires to inspire you to leave a legacy of family, adventure, relationships, health and joy. Life really is sweeter with honey. You can visit her at www.LegacyofJoyInc.com.